I0143065

SHARING LOVE

A selection of Sam's Poems

Poetry – "The passion and the Pain"

Published by Personal Publishing New Zealand 2016

This edition of Sam's Poems was produced and published in
Aotearoa New Zealand 2016

ISBN 978-0-473-37885-1

Copies may be obtained through Amazon and the following
website or email address

www.poems-by-sam.com
sam@poems-by-sam.com

Personal Publishing
PO Box 15071
Tauranga, 3144 New Zealand

Copyright Agency Viscopy
Level 11, 66 Goulburn Street, Sydney NSW 2000
www.copyright.com.au   www.viscopy.org.au

Note from the Author Sam Eastwood

When I sit and write I find the words come into existence as a journal entry, a poem, verse, rhyme or short essay. They are a reflection of the unfolding mystery of my life, interwoven into the present associated feelings and emotions I'm experiencing they thread through and tie my life's path together.

My poems are about love and the feelings and emotions love brings to us, and are strongly influenced by my spirituality.
I have refined these poems with the help of my editor Shona-Ellen Barnett, to frame the picture I paint with my words. I would also like to acknowledge my graphic designer Rebecca Larsen for her assistance, and give thanks to all the people who helped with this selection, for their critique, suggestions and the poems they enjoyed reading from my other books titled, *Sam's Poems I, Sam's Poems II and Sam's Poems III. Love Poèmes & Érotique verse.*

Poems published in other media
The Australia Times Poetry magazine
A printed anthology by Allpoetry.com
The Tuck magazine online publication UK 2016
Three poems translated in Serbian, published in literary blogs and in Serbian printed magazines 2016.

PREFACE

It is a privilege for me to introduce Sam Eastwood's poetry.
He writes with wonderful control, passionately and
expressively about love in its many and varied
manifestations, so that each poem is unique, emotionally
intense and engaging.
The title, 'Sharing Love' represents the relationship between
Sam and his readers, which is intimate and personal, so that
the poetry, Sam and the reader, are united in the joys of
communication and collaboration.

Ken W Simpson,
My latest collection, Patterns of Perception, was published
by Augur Press (UK) in 2015.
I write under the name of Ken W Simpson, an Australian
poet.

My Poetry

Poems are like pictures
seen in the mind

Words are emotions
waiting to be explored

Poems are feelings
coming to mind

Words linger
thoughts open the door

Poems free imagination
an inclination to see
within and without
the play of life.

INDEX

To Critique life	1
A wakeful dance at dawn	2
An innocent time	3
Be with Me	4
Forlorn Shadows	5
Love	7
Sateen Sheets	8
A question I asked of me, within	9
Accepting	10
I AM.	11
Never in a million years	12
On a winters day	13
To Sam – Cecile's poem	15
Sometimes	16
Warm in your arms	17
The night train called Desire	19
Passion	20
Sunset reflections	21

Snowflakes   22

Lovers gift to each other   23

Ripples   24

Heaven's door (*new version*)   25

Awareness   27

Raindrops, puddles   28

The Temple of Tranquillity   29

Without prejudice & Expecting nothing   30

Upon the Stage of life   31

Waiting   33

February in May   34

Oceans of awareness   35

I desire   36

Immeasurable   37

Lost? & Found !   38

Continues   40

Meditation Our Breath IN   41

Inspired by the 23rd Psalm   42

We breathe   43

Dust   44

Letter to a Soulmate   45

The beauty of inner being   46

A description of Demoiselle Qi   47

The Matrix of Demoiselle Qi   48

Sunshine   49

For the Lover   50

Then there is this   51

The Citadel   52

Reflections II   53

Leaves Fall   54

MELding into light Blues of desire.   55

Melting   57

Autumn   58

Autumn's sweet rhyme   60

Lelia's poem   61

Spellbinder   63

The warmth of your smile   64

Although   65

The stairway to the stars   66

I wander as I wonder   67

XXX   68

My Muse   69

The Birthday Balloon Tree   70

For a Birthday   71

Interconnected   72

Enlightened   73

"When we change the way we think, it changes the way we feel, so we understand who we are"

To Critique Life

"What's true
is in front of us
we move towards it
even though we don't
know it's there." Walt Whitman

Once you have come to know
where you came from
aware of reason,
you will walk
the earth with understanding.

Your eyes gazing
into the heaven
out there among the stars
our interconnectedness unfolds
wisdom and love
our peaceful journey.

A wakeful dance at dawn

Timeless is a place
where dreams are born
it warms the heart of the sun.

Stardust rests on eyelids
heavy with slumber.
Mistress morning
lights Love in our being

Wandering new destinations
imagination kindles a restless yearning
for love's wisdom surrounding
our heart with joy
soft pleasures this mystery

Inclination pulls the sheets from overhead
we rise to begin a new day of gifts
peaceful grace to etch the space
love held within

Soulful emotions
weave seamless rhythms
an endless presence
another day filled with love
never lost.

An innocent time

Dressed in openness we invite
in madness
To feel again and let emotions
to escape and enjoy once more

You invite me to enter knowing
I am willing

We move the line, "just friends"
a little, each time, just a little more
"It's fine."
Who will be the first say, "I want you?"
Each hopes the other will, Waiting.

We feel more, not less, inner
knowing where this may lead
I ask, "am I off the track?"

The line fades
this point is reached
We enjoy moments
both dreaming
How far I have slipped?
A whisper, an embrace
two hearts are filled
passion charged
The beginning or other end?
we say, "We are just good friends"

Be with Me

I hold the flaming torch
burning my Soul
it's desire, Love

Reaches out to me,
your Soul evokes a response
lingering close
your heart opens, seeking

A collision,
solitude bursts into radiance
a kaleidoscope of pattern
rhythm and enlightenment
in consciousness

Words of love
longings shared
doors open.
Spirit meets love's intent
walking slowly
we touch hands
and hold

Hearts, gentleness
and grace, love kindles
the reality of our
open faithful sincerity

Lips kiss, we are
the fragrance of life, infused
our souls create moments
of mystery and magic.

Forlorn Shadows

Lovers hand-in-hand
shape gaze

Clouds billow
edges of grey
shape shifting patterns
ominous. The picnickers
go home, forlorn.

Darkness invades sun rays
cold feelings
foretell emptiness
Emotions descend before
a darkening of premise

A flash of light
blackness thunders
and resonates the soul
descends into despair

No flame in the torch
the inner ache of the heart
clings to hope
flailed by the lure of love

A vast void spews
eternal malice
on thine inner faith
of a reprobate's poor soul
hope cries
and dies.

No redemption
No grace
No heaven
The despair
of a place warmed
by Hell.

"I love our planet, and hope this is not our swansong"

LOVE

Love the Universal Consciousness
Love God dwelling within us
Love our meaning of life

Love unfathomable
Love intangible
Love the magic

Love non-judgemental
Love doubtless
Love painless

Love brings Joy
Love brings Hope
Love brings Peace

Love our creation
Love our beauty of feeling
Love our hearts shared

Love is acceptance
Love is grace
Love is wisdom.

In the eternal, love unfolds out to us, which we give back to all
living sentient Beings, our interconnectedness to this Life.

Sateen Sheets

Kisses in the park, of soulfulness and essence
as lover's embrace, fleeting glimpses of desires
lips tingling with excitement, awaiting passion

Lives finding newness, freedom waiting expression.
soft silky voices whisper offers, the melodies linger
wild fingers caressing, as lovers dance intimately

Gazing, glassy water filled eyes, our lovers in Nirvana
unbound, a poetry of feelings and sensations
both hearts seductively entwined, exploring tenderness

Movements and songs play on these lovers meadow.
their breathless sighs echo, weaving love's creation
dreams unfolding, sleeping together within Sateen
sheets.

*Published in The Australia Times Poetry Magazine
vol 4 no.12 June 2016*

A question I asked

As your heart touched mine I considered
accepting you fully and faithfully

I asked myself, "How deep is love?"
and a spirit arose to explain

To begin rest in sincerity
and truthfulness

Freedom begins with "what we say"
from a heart without conditions

Choose free will, to be faithful,
free from ego

Conscious enlightenment
the rhythm of true love

Creation vibrates our expression
each moment accepting
without prejudice & expecting nothing.

But to be free souls who share this
path we walk.

Accepting

So long, ever so long
this ache has invaded my mind
numbing my heart

This journey of awaking,
I plead "Why does it not come to me
Weightless?"

I am a prisoner
chained to a damp wall
emotions robed in endless tatters

Understanding with acceptance
inner strength and wisdom
alights my consciousness
Awareness, letting go

Grace with Love.

*According to Plato's Socrates, the shadows on the wall of a cave
are as close as the prisoners get to viewing reality. He then
explains how the philosopher is like a prisoner who is freed from
the cave and comes to understand that the shadows on the wall do
not make up reality at all, as he can perceive the true form of
reality rather than the mere shadows seen by the prisoners.*

I AM

I am the wind in your hair
I am the sun warming your body

I am the rain dancing on your face
I am the snowflakes drifting the air

I am the flowers sending their fragrance upward
I am the air

I am the beginning of your first thought
I am the end of your last

I am the idea sparking your most brilliant
I am the glory of fulfilment

I am the feeling
you who yearns

(Do this in remembrance of me)

*Inspired by the book "Conversations with God" by
Neale Donald Walsch
And my beliefs in Conscious awaking – "Create and you
will be me as I am you"*

Translated in Serbian, and published in literary blogs.

Never in a trillion years

You are in a place never imagined
days drift dream-like
Work, appointments, nights alone
filled with memories of love
never forever

A canvas of colour,
brushed with heavenly strokes
glistens with beauty,
radiating
how love was and should be,
now turned to the wall

Unexpectedly Cupid's
impossible arrow

Your kiss of light
the joy of closeness
Our awakening
our spirits, faithful
deepening.

Never in a trillion years, imagined,
a reunion
a pathway of hope, happiness
Souls embracing,
a peaceful acceptance, just us.

For all lovers finding each other

A winter's day

My laptop slumbers
key's white letters worn
fading shiny brown
once elegant

Soulful without much to do
I sit staring at this
wondering once was
no more a mere tool

Many play games
surf, read the news
a strange sense of serenity
comes to me, I don't know

You may feel the same
maybe the answer lies within
a mix of feelings
some we don't understand

One of loss, another like standing
in a long queue not moving
then there's this over-thinking
I can't stop

Turning the corner I hope to lose
this trail of thoughts only to find
another just around the next bend
All of which is to no
avail

I am loosing the 'me' I once understood
A new chapter has begun
the main character who I thought
I was, no longer appears

The story line is a blur
despite my clear vision
the last chapters, I am in these
filled with questionable confidence

Serenity, now familiar
that's all there is Now!

Published in The Australia Times Poetry Magazine vol 4 no.12
June 2016

To Sam

My Soul calls to you across the chasm
Of my own making
Yet there is no other
Who could understand
The call of my heart
Torn apart

Yet you have heard the call of your own Soul
To love without condition
To allow another to walk her path
Freely
Without limits
In love unbounded
Knowingly accepting the pain of letting go

Greater love hath no man
Than to set another free
In abiding love
Your love for me

Your Princess

A poem selected by a friend as one I should include in this
publication, with the writer's permission.

Sometimes

Sometimes our love defeats our lust, but sometimes not
Sometimes our peace is kept by trust, but sometimes not

Sometimes we are hurt and held and healed
Sometimes we share heart and mind, but sometimes not

Sometimes we are lost lovers, our lives blaze with
bursts of passion, but sometimes not

Sometimes we are best friends, we balance compassion
and love, but sometimes not

Sometimes we are up-in-arms night and day, our battles
are fought and lost, but sometimes not

Sometimes we are at-loose-ends and struggle to be one
with ourselves, but sometimes not

Sometimes we are with others entertaining family
and friends, but sometimes not

Sometimes we are you and me, keeping good company
but, sometimes not

*A rewritten amalgamation from an anonymous poem and by
me.*

"Sometimes the veil or mask we wear cannot conceal how we truly feel and our emotions are freed from where the heart too often hides"

Warm in your arms

Love holds, awaking in drowsiness
I brush your cheek with my fingers, your lips
alight my day as we whisper to each other, love

The days are gone, since you passed
I am numb, a little tired, each day filled
pompous needs and hurry. Floating I dream

I visit where we walked; familiar sounds
coffee at the table where we talked, bustling streets
the evenings we made love by the fire

My emotions well up, I wonder why
we were placed to ever have met;
You cast love aside, left me adrift with no shore

What gain to those whose heart is scarred?
Years slip by in timeless fashion. Others say
time to move on "To where?" I reply

No resolution comes to soothe this soul
minutes, hours, days drift by. Continual, uninvolved
troubled, this unrelenting journey I now face

Loneliness cripples my will
a yearning not to be like this

I pick my heart from the floor
new-found grace and peace lighten the load
in the Wisdom I have known true love.

"To have loved and lost is better than to have never loved at all"
Maybe? maybe not!... I put on my mask, to hide away these
things, my outer world has not time for.

The night train called Desire

It begins simply
a glassy glassed haze
a match, struck
to kindle a blaze

Streams of hissing steam
gauges measures pleasure
relay important messages
to engage, treasure

Loosed to the wheels
Sighing, skidding,
shudders, jostling
spinning, for traction

Slowly, there's movement
progress applauds gentle force
increasing motion builds
pleasing rhythms on course

A journey unfolding
destination excites
reverberations beating the gaps
musical wheels and rails unite

A climax
caresses, stokes a fire
tender, lingers with Love
releasing all traveler's desires.

Passion

I begin, I make no excuse
to ignite your imagination
to set your soul ablaze
to consume you with desire
Passion on fire

Don't cry into emptiness
no one will listen to your sadness
the past I've ripped away
your future is beginning
take a chance, hold me close
I'll show you the magic of love

My candle of hope
will not be extinguished
I will crush your fears
take darkness from your soul
Look, feel, believe. Can you
offer me your wild passion?

Do you doubt me?
Test my love with your heart
I'll arouse your exotic fantasies
fill your erotic demands
Know you'll never need
Forgiveness

Understand freedom
but if your mind is set-
with my heart
I'll see you fly away
Free

Sunset reflections

A kaleidoscope of gold
bronze and pink-blue hues
upon wind rippled waters
wash the unlocked sea
of illumination

Surreal the old twisted
Pohutukawa; resting in line
near the bleached sand
sun-scorched baches
park close one to another
red tin roofs, weathered fences

A lover's lane awaits
those tempted to explore
the magic of this path
a carpet of autumn gold
leaves waltz
in the gentle breeze

Evening orchestra of birds
sing their young to sleep
Places like this, to belong
mindful, gifted and aware
opens our mind
to a reflective day

I slip on my robe
to wander these shores
Love
the endearment
of this extraordinary world.

* Bach is a New Zealand term for a small beach cottage

Snowflakes

Summertime hibernates to sleep away the cold
Kindled oak crackling into embers
an evening mood brings thoughts of you again
Loving you by my side, dreams filled with summer
picnics, sausages, children playing in the sun

Wild winter winds roar through the trees
thunderous white-caps crash upon the shore
Sun-filtered mist halos of beautiful design
Snowflakes whisper to the grey skies
Here we are, finding warmth cuddled together

New snow rests upon the sill from its journey,
forming a pattern of crystal wonder,
flakes together where they found each other.
Is it by mindless folly or design we came here?
filled with anticipation, to celebrate life

Where a blanket of white, a carrot-nose snowman
tipping black hat, skaters on a lake of ice
red wine, black coffee, chocolate steaming hot
Sunrise enshrines the still air, I take your hand,
a snowflake a kiss.

Lovers gift to each other

Soft breezes whisper around silk shades
Dawn's light washes a star-filled sky

Crystal sheets wrap longing lovers close
Drowsy kisses, tender lips caress

Sunrays infuse the air with love's fragrance
Umbrellas shade urban cafés, lovers' nests

Roasted aromas, Caribbean bean, dry red grape
Hands touching, holding, toes kissing shoes

Gazes, smiles, lips muse before yielding
Passionate embraces under the Elms.

Dusk, heaven's magical twilight, stars serenade
Pillow mounds, damp silk a tangled canopy veil

Lovers gift each other's deepest sensual excitement
Desires explode beneath a bedcover of enticement

Souls become timeless, eternal; locked in
Togetherness.

Published in print, 'Remembering Spring' a poem anthology by Allpoetry.com 2016

Ripples

A speck of stardust
existing within eternity
finds the other speck
and invites a reality

Ripples, waves crisscross
mindfulness explored
reflecting on the surface
our being, non-clinging

Dreams interrupt
resting in stillness
thoughts arise as emotions
form words, to become

Deeper into the pond
silence between words
drops fall, meets surface
ripples waves crisscross

Interconnectedness is born
peaceful wisdom, resting
the first breath taken in
air breathed, slowly out

Enlightenment our mother
Illumination our father
Compassion our will
Love our undertaking

Heaven's Door

Softly lapping the shores of dreams
wondering emotions lost in time
reveal endless wandering
arriving nowhere. Now
a herald brings news
of the door that awaits

Tender lips grace mine
a love laced with hope
a magic affliction
Leaves falling
charting another life
losing all desires

Arriving at this doorstep
graceful hearts stand
not of thou beliefs
nor understanding
this doorway to cross
A question asked,
without presumption

Frail souls wait outside
with no answer
Saints gather with love
faithfulness gains admittance
once thrice tried true love
eternal wings lift away
steadfast mortal character

We stand, a reputation
knocking loud
an endless reverberation.
Faith forever echoes,
an omnipresent eternity
that offers peace
without cost or price
freedom, love overflowing

Through this door we pass
to love unconditionally.

Awareness

Fulfilling connections
understanding freedom
sharing universal wisdom

To feel inspired
loving, gracious
and belonging

Accepting guidance
within mindfulness
with interconnectedness

Dwelling in the presence
every breath
every present moment
Alive

A gift to replenish
to enrich
each other in consciousness

Translated in Serbian, and published in literary blogs.

**Raindrops, puddles,
a wandering mind.**

Raindrops splash puddles
upon my terrace
grey clouds drift by
reflections in little ponds

Ripples race to the edge
before the next drop falls
from heaven
where in my mind
I wander though dreams

A moment stills
opening gaps
soon filled, thinking
truth may be the ripple
that tests my beliefs
"Love is the meaning of life"

Emotions persist
when they're not free
to fly with grace,
glowing with elegance
rain drops dancing
ripples on puddles

I drift to Now
where forever is stored
with peaceful exuberance
abandonment of thoughts
in this place, Now I abide.

The Temple of Tranquillity

In the Temple of Tranquillity
I rest in peacefulness
'Now' its presence
silence a residence
in Consciousness

From infinity
our being is formed
embedded in wisdom
experiencing perfection
the path of life

Transcendent Truth
love for all beings
non-Self in virtue encounters
the Buddha's
heavenly grace

Formless, desire less
fragrant the
Mindfulness

Practising the Way
guarded the soul
abiding right thought
purified, transparent
Nirvana eternal.

Inspired by the teachings of Buddha

Without prejudice & expecting nothing

I wander along
my little path of life, oblivious
Sometimes stopping,
feeling a breeze of wonderment
touch my soul, lightly

Here I found you, looking
wandering your own path
stopping from time to time
Bewilderment touches your soul
with unknown cause

Meeting somehow extraordinary
least expected, letting time unveil
a mystery so transparent
tugging our awareness, seeking
without prejudice, expecting nothing

You and me find
an incredible radiance
touches our earthly form
We go along knowing it's begun
giving everything we thought lost.

Upon the Stage of life

A hot summer breeze passing
a path spilt with tables and chairs
Together, sharing knowing glances
your enticing voice a soft melody

Sitting under umbrellas sipping Bubbles
the participants upon the stage drift by
Our words, jingle our life story
senses tingle to your perfume

I watch you with fascination, lips smiling
eyes that dream of Prada, shoes and bags
Our fellowship I miss whenever away
I'm lapping up today

Passing lovers gliding hand in hand
an impetuous kiss she plants on his cheek
a surprise he tries to hide, hoping for more
We surmise she does this often, to note

Waitress Ellie, our pizza arrives
Nearby a group, joining tables and chairs
another wondering party stops to laze
girls sitting, Rose glasses holding hair

Children eating ice cream as parents wait
dreaming of holidays by the beach
Poodles, straw-hats, roll sleeves, cigars
the passing sidewalk melodies

Guys fashion jeans, peruse girls in bikinis
Life, living for today, looking for each other
Mid afternoon sitting together to gossip
later the beach, and wet toes

A moonlit sky, damp lips dancing tangos
Playmating.

Waiting

I fall asleep in darkness
it comes so quick
I feel no fear
waiting for the day
I'll meet you

Dreams of newness and wonder
tender feelings of closeness
True love I understand
never to lose, waiting

Today a new beginning
Of yesterday nothing remains,
Change brings understanding
What I fear, waiting too long

I am lost in the day, work
engaged in mind and body
Time stands still or rushes by
the day spent waiting

Laying waiting sleeping
was that all today?
Falling into my dream
there again, Together

No waiting on this day
the miracle's closer
your arrival
the departure of waiting

February in May

Windy weather blows good news & Blues
Sunshine, baked apple pie and cream

Cloudy puffs passing summer heat
grey heavens dancing raindrop's Tango

May's beautiful princess, dancers swirling,
shifting by weeping willow

Meditation of mindfulness, everything love
golden leaves, weaving spells all day

May with February, wand in hand meddling
with you and me, an artistic spell

Love is you and me sharing
sunsets and horizons, building new days

Roses, the fragrance of our dreams
Imaginations wander, taking you with me.

Oceans of awareness

On the vast Ocean of Conscious Tranquility
which reflects the light of illumination
I look at the shore lost in wonder
the sun's brilliance shared with the moon
little ripples washing the shore
each loving creation gifts to our soul

Slowly wandering my path of life
that which I am, Now, learning every step
this beautiful experience I am creating
with the Universal consciousness
Love is unfolding awaking me
causes me to turn and see

There is another, barefoot
drifting slowly to me.
Filled with radiance, knowing enters
together we are both teacher and student
She stands beside me in presence
without speaking taking each other's hand
knowing we were nowhere, Now here

Our desire Enlightenment
gifted universal awareness
to experience unconditional love
Love is free will
power to always to heal
We walk an unknown future
one we create in every moment
Hope filled with Joy as One.

I desire

to feel you tremble with joy
to be there when you laugh
to be there when you feel sad
to be there when you cry

for the pleasure of your company
for you to feel loved
for you to feel my Love
for you to be safe

to never cause you hurt
to be with you
to be beside you
to hold you in my arms

And help you, to always be You

Immeasurable

Light filters into my room
a new day unfolds
Our love comes into my thoughts
filling me with anticipation

This wonderful emotion, softly your name
into the air as if you're here
Warmth surrounds love's touch
when we are together

Your hand captured in mine, we walk
brushing hair from your cheek, we kiss
Lips tremble as they touch
pulling us close, and closer

Now to explore

Where Love grows, yet is immeasurable
Love brings hope beyond expectation
Love can move the whole universe

Where Love is, time never touches
Love forms the union in each other's soul
Love is you and me together

"These days I wish for you."

Lost

I lay gazing into heaven's beautiful light
feeling the gift of creation kiss my thoughts
Such a wonder. Yet! Unknown peace
colliding stars, wrenching moons into planets
billowing clouds of meteor radiation dust
imploding down black holes of hunger.
What is left of time, this infinite all?

I look to the sea, dawn to day
waves wash life, smooth the sand
Was something written there?
Land born new with life and hope
Taken by thrust of dead deeds and misery
over turned, cut, divided, barren stripped
wasted, always sold with greed

I had love, a song locked
within my heart, wings around my soul
reaching out, no other to comprehend
Life lost animation, greasy, greedy grime
Dark, cold nothingness, filled with pain
never time to try again
what heart is left for this man

This poem won third place from 26 entries, in a competition run
by a member of Allpoerty.com 24th October 2016

& Found

She is light, a wonder of creation
to hold my thought
removing my unknown peace
Stars, planets, dancing lovers, Moon
I give to love my infinite all

With dawn, her washing my life
kindness into my spirit with hope
Born a new trust to love
unconditional love given
I can feel what was written

Life's presence our spirit and soul
reaching deep into our hearts
for all that may understand
We need to try to in love again

And understand our Earth.

Continues

I gave little and received so much.
Finding feeling within a dream
I lost yesterday

Today continues my search
a new beginning
a lightness of soul
Time I have
to look for you.

Translated in Serbian, and published in literary blogs.

Meditation
Our breathe

In

Celestial soulfulness lights love in our breath
a mind full of thoughts begins to slumber
drifting, presence comes, then resides
Peacefulness within

Out

The current of love's breath runs deep
watching thinking, have its dreams
Serenely the practice of Breathe

In

Heaven's choir announces the truth
another breath, we chant, emancipation,
the wonder of creation's love
aware of selflessness, grace settles
our soul, renewed with each breathe taken

Out

our being freed from endless thoughts
elation fills our Soul, in the Now.

Universal consciousness
is my guide, so I create.

I walk

by the oceans of serenity
in the presence
of universal grace.

Consciousness restores my soul
to peace.
I am led by faith and truth.

With love
I face shadows in the void.
I will myself
to hold no fear or hate.

True to my being, forever
in this presence;
Enlightenment and illumination
before me.

Anointed and comforted with hope,
my days filled
with unconditional love;
I dwell in this form
that I am given.

Inspired by the 23rd Psalm

We breathe

We breathe in, soft as silk
inner translucent radiance
air passing delicate lips
as lovers first kiss

We breathe out a beauty rich
to nature in truth and purity
air passing delicate lips
evocative, a perfume rose

We breathe in, inner stillness
willingness opens out to life
air passing delicate lips
a love of peace, felt inside

We breathe out with fullness
of hope and reflection
air passing delicate lips
freedom from non-clinging

Our breathe caresses meaning
forever, an infinite wish
air passing delicate lips
we reach a new beginning.

Dust

A letter about dust,
or flecks in a light wind
In my heart I have no lust

Dust makes my heart less able
to feel free, right and stable
to witness our beautiful world

Light fills my heart with love
life ascends as a peaceful dove
dusting away in my heart

Dusting away, shifting the sad
trails of memory good or bad
sometimes love has a little dust

Love is whole, and coming to us
special friends dusting thus
along and around, this Paradise

With a fleeting glimpse of you,
you doing the same! Seeing me
dusting around inside the heart

Dusting away, and finding us

Letter to a Soulmate

To a Soulmate, my connection with another
enlightened, aware of the meaning to all life

Unintentional, without anticipation, natural, truthful
in creation, without prejudice, in our Souls

Together, walking in alliance, loving
unconditionally a shared pathway to understanding

In the peacefulness of silence we abide
gifting each other illumination and knowledge

Letting the Universal Consciousness experience
itself through all we create. Hope, wisdom, and
faithfulness

Perfect Love, unfolds in us and ripples on the
oceans of awareness, washing the shores of
'Presence'

We experience feeling and emotions being
intrinsically human, sharing love's beautiful
physical intimacy

Free in our will for each other, to be ourselves,
aware our differences yet completely One with the
Creation.

The beauty of interbeing

The external world may not see
how it is for you and me.

I hold a vision
another soul close to mine
to share, giving from within
together we listen,
to gather understanding

Our thirst to experience
the inner glow,
an insight of each other

Engaged in reality
your soul contacts mine
embracing mindfulness
elucidating incandescence
within kindred spirits

Life's beauty is reflected
to the external world
of empathy
intuitiveness,
so graced to create

A reality of simplicity
steeped in wisdom
unfolding awareness
the exquisite,
meaning and sharing of life.

A description of
Demoiselle Qi

A very interesting woman, (Dangerous)
A beautiful young lady entrancing, (Deadly)
The fascinating slayer of men's will, (Lethal)

Empowered within expression, (Delightful)
Exquisitely unbound sensuality, (Desirable)

Gifted by the morning Star
his creation Qi
A Majae

She speaks with a, "Hey U" (Heavenly)
a smile melts with tenderness and immanence
Deep brown eyes, captivating; (erotic)

Damp lips wait to kiss you.

To be contd,

The Matrix of Demoiselle Qi

Soul so u-fur-mystic.
wandering suggestions
so deeply true
steeped in consequences

Locked in dreams
belief in magic
seats mystical desire
experimentations, exquisiteness

Now standing waiting
at the door of Love
the mixing of genes
miracle curers

Follow me always
here in the Revolution
wondrous twists of Faith
innocence Denied

Here, I stand and knock
pleasures echo around
mysterious companion take me
and cover me with pure light

Race me now, encase me now
Embrace me now, with your LOVE.

For the waitress of De'vil Cafe

Sunshine

Her song, low and mellow
a soft wet Sunshine.
Fulfilling a tantalizing breeze
lovemaking
Delicate caresses, her wonder
a fragrance, as dawn's early bouquet
surrenders

To hold her within my arms
as fingers intertwine with mine
Little looks leaping from desire
lips kiss, pleasure with presence
Sunshine's thighs a silk pink glow
Her sighs linger on murmuring breath

A beauty, a peaceful expression
Cascading rhythms at arousal's peak
Love soulful and unselfish finds
tenderness within our sensual being
Rushing as both heartbeats race
plosion, united together; Orgasm

Laying together, in caresses
sweet oils' perfume
Lips melting, a satin pleasure
oneness in our togetherness
then resting, drifting into dreams
lingering under the shades

Sunshine a soft breeze from heaven
Fire of Earth, light of moon
the redolence of life, our Love.

For the lover...

So beautiful a lady
filled with life, with joy

Eyes, bright with love
understanding, patient

Auburn, a small waterfall
flows dancing with every tone.

Lips soft and warm
a heart the same

A will all your own, not strong
to listen, determined the same

Belief in the hardness of life
gentle for those of lesser means

Not filled with your own dreams
to see them in others

Then there is this

I am a very happy dreamer

I have a few things, however, I need to do:
One to decide where to go; Two with Whom

Is Love not for us to choose?
a relationship, not wanting to lose

Walking graciously through future blues
I look at our stars, majestic signs in hues

Feeling you're my answer, the One and Two
I'm with love, waiting, here for you.

The Citadel

Outwards runs time, slips into the night
the moon stands still, seeking the sun
Forever in the blink of an eye, comes Creation

The Bell of Heaven stands quiet. Silence said,
"Love is life, forever eternal" It rings loud,
echoing undulations of possibilities, Life begins

Defining the will of the singularity; Love's birth
released consequences, one true Consciousness
immortal becomes mortal living in love

In an age of reason, yes there's indecision
casting lots, wishing the game to begin
waiting willfully to start
Love rests in the Citadel

The battle was Hers (as True Love knows)
This time she caught and spun until withered-
Life is the possibility of you and me.

Reflections II

Grey skies winter hues
puddles on deck railings
shimmer to the winds will
Sunlight reflections gather on my wall
thoughts of love, dancing with Desires

Raindrops purge the image
hallows of light, patchwork emotions
Life sings love my thoughts
willing away my haze
Lazy afternoon daydreams of you

Winter hues pale,
Love tingles me, I feel close
your smile as we meet, "ciao"
French kisses; every hug a melody
lingering, sinuously making Love

Dancing reflections
on my wall

Leaves Fall

Alone with a Lover

Enfolded we are together
Cherry blossom lays a silken carpet
along the lovers lane.
Nothing less than exceptional
you fill my life with Spring

The air is alive
fairies travel to magic,
hearts softly joining together
two souls filled with presence, Awake
(Enlightenment opens)

Longing,
feelings envelope, passion
Lips silky dampness, stirs foundations
Making love.

Melding

Melding into light Blues of desire

I see her often, smiles and impressions
happy, confident, a little girl there too
Essence of woman, giggles and frowns
catching my glance
darker outer edge, a glassy glitter
How wonderful to gaze upon
Melding into her light Blues

Watching clouds weaving by

Friendship, openly desiring to be her lover
whatever her journey, a path beside her
imagination, illuminations and, dreams
What is in her light-filled eyes? Love and faith
reflecting her amassment of life's wonders
Holding hands, connected with her
Melding into her light Blues

Moonlit skies and stars made for Lovers

Sharing existences, merging understanding
being with her in a garden of mindfulness
Loving embraces, French kisses & togetherness
presence, feelings wrapped with soulfulness
Heart-filled emotions, captivating her love
finding each other. Making Love and
Melding into her light Blues

Like the Sun, warming a winter's day, as Spring

Sleeping with a Tsunami of wild emotions
hair spilling over pillows. Soft songs of sleep
awakening with a gift from Heaven. Lips
transform
a gentle sigh, kisses herald a new day
An Angel snuggling close
this wondrous moment, just to be
Melding into her light Blues.

Melting

Lashed by heaving emotional waves
waves that ebb and flow, washing over me
As a tide of strong rhythm, deep currents
pound beautiful white sand
I'm part of this nature, and you're belonging

I choose to be myself, and then you visit me
accepting this newness we grow closer
Time the animistic, flows in my awareness
Souls feel love's animation, touching revelations
freedom to explore our climactic experience

Melting away the ICE, becoming Me with You
Magical miracles grow, becoming alive
Poems émouvoir; empathy in me and you
Love's sensual emotions, endearments revealed
tangible these moments here together

I live with passion, the excitement of you
no longer sentimental, foolishness gone
Free falling surrender, accepting change, and loss
Wisdom, insight, giving without receiving
Being Me. Being You, events without time,

Three poems about autumn

Autumn

Autumn leaves turn gold
dance across my path
the lane stretches ahead
beyond softness without feeling
a touch without depth
close yet strange

My brave heart
still wants togetherness
but there is nothing more
a distance perceived
all is lost

Falling into the enthralling void
your essence flows from every pore
You are my captivation
my long desire

We had Love where emotion
and expression were free
except you untied everything

You needed this that I understand
But you gave up your freedom

To chains of another's desire.

Autumn cont...

All my caresses of love
willingly turned aside
though they were the very thing
that set you free

Another rusted soul not yours
gestured to me accusing
then demanding some reprisal
for satisfaction

Bizarre I do understand
and knew from the start
but here from there and where?
Did it matter my love?

Yes thoughts locked in
losing you to love another
my heart becoming free
letting Be.

Autumn's sweet rhyme

Yellow leaves
raindrops dancing in rows
falling, the wind blows

Grey skies threaten
air brisk, a cold chill,
coat, scarf and gloves

A lane stretches ahead
along this path wondering
along this path wandering

Excited to return home,
hot tea with croissants
and writing about the sun

We gather undercover
nicely huddled together
out of the weather.

Without you

Without you I am lost
a life lost of objective
sensations I never felt before
I needed no one

But then I have you
I feel empty and alone
with you I don't know fantasy
I feel no reality

I see your face and yet
lack everything, a dream
I lay awake, eyes open
I can't move onward

My heart full of anguish
without reason?
So I suffer for your love
not having you and...

At the same time having you
within my soul
within me.
I wish you here forever now

I would give all
to have you by my side
 I wish to give you as much
as much as love would

You within my skin
so when your name
is spoken by another
I shiver

So that you know I exist
I cry that nobody can love you as me
But it has to be this way
in such a distant place

I rest that you should not be different
from any other people
That you for any reason
you could find out

I am waiting for you
waiting the occasion
for our encounter
Of a friend.

Poem from a pen friend in Argentina
Lelia, said it was about her Lover who left her without a word.

SPELLBINDER

Merlin
invoking the universe's unfathomable mystery
The Angel of the Lord came from the mists of time
to rebuke those of unholy deeds, and spirits
Seventy-seven saintly monks attended
the unbroken pentagram, demons rendered
powerless

Merlin, wizard, spellbinder of the White Light
stood on holy ground engaging with the alliance
Shadow Catcher, holder of life's Gemstone
Princess of the dark moors, the oracle of knowing
The Black Shadow, holder of the Twilight Sword
The Magi gathered for the awakening of the
Archangel

Love, faithfulness and truth, bestowed wisdom
filled the soul of the Celestial Being
and the Archangel took physical form.

The warmth of your smile

The gentle warmth of your smile
permeates the seat of my soul
the seed of love which has lain
deeply in my being for eons
grows within my heart
filling me with peace and joy

As your teacher I give you nothing
but speak to what you already have
for the truth to penetrate
for your full understanding
and to water the seeds
of your own Enlightenment

As your lover,
you gave me everything
but not your heart
which belongs to another
Now freed from this desire
my life regains meaning

A sunset kiss
rests upon my lips

When emotions take over from our reality and intuition

Although

Although I have not read The Book
I have an intuitive empathy for the story
I feel the sadness
I live with this
in my house of love

Do we live in a materialistic world
with immoral values, lustful
and with utter greed?

If so, who stands up
To draw a line in the sand
and says no more?

I do.

The Stairway to the Stars

The flute calls, a stairway through the Stars
I linger, losing myself in the openness
my life's path unfolding
in silence my heart sings

I am filled with light, and understanding.
Love and truth invade me
I wander my path living in wonder
thinking of you, wishing to hold you again
No burden, love's acceptance, Free

No words, no sound elaborates,
my thoughts unconditional with acceptance
change, impermanence. As days linger
slipping by, I take up my ocean of faith
spring clean, time to sit and meditate

The road calls you to join
can you feel the breeze
calling you to where this stairway lies
whispering winds carry your light
let Love fill all hearts, gently free

Waking up in the morning, I smile
Twenty four brand new hours ahead
I vow to live fully in each moment,
with eyes of Love.

I wander as I wonder

How did end up here
it's late and nowhere

Feelings drift
decisions await answers
choices await outcomes

The silent scream
of impossible solutions
grasp nothing
in absent presence
lost to the deafening quiet

Like resident aliens
in conspicuous absence
unconscious awareness
the forgotten past
of the future

From life's magic
we meander to
death's song
an ageless time
joined unattached

I'm conscious of truth
in this masquerade
"Awake Soul being"
We're not alone together
the oxymoron in our creation
joyful pain, Love from hurt.

*A poem to celebrate life in all its ups and downs an oxymoron
others would have us believe that we can't create our own
destiny, we do*

XXX

As she was about to orgasm
husband finished
made a sandwich

When she is about to orgasm
Lover plays the precise cord
Exquisite shared climax

My muse

Looking at the Milky Way
I see you

Looking at the stars
I see you

Being alive on this beautiful planet
with you

Holding the wisdom
I share with you

Knowing the faithfulness
I share with you

To be gracefully
in spirit with you

To discover home
finding you

Being together
holding you

Sharing the desires
within you

Explored emotions, spoken truths
the door to freedom.

Serendipity

Joyful and soulfulness

The Birthday Balloon Tree

This story is not about the tree
it's about Samuel.

He is a very strange little boy
and he's very clever too
Samuel is an inventor; he makes things that fly
He grows strange trees that bloom balloons
only on Birthdays

Samuel likes most things
Brussel Sprouts, Tripe
and warm Ice Cream
But most of all, he likes his trees
with large Balloons
of multi-coloured strips
curls and whorls
that stay a while
then drift away

I've not seen him for a long time
but if you'd like
one of his special trees
that bloom with balloons
in your choice of colours
multi coloured strips
curls and whorls
on your birthday

Then let me know
I'll ask him the next time
he comes to have Brussel Sprouts
Tripe and warm Vanilla Ice Cream
with me.

For 'add name'*

To celebrate your creation,
a beautiful life brought into being
from the stardust at the beginning
of the timeless Universe
May you be enriched with wisdom
endowed with universal consciousness
and your Soul be forever replenished

Happy Birthday

"May your faithfulness in love never end,
no matter where life's path may take you

Love

Will endure for eternity".

* You have my permission to use this poem for someone you love
as long as you note it was written by Sam's poems©

Interconnected

In the natural flow of what is occurring

co-emerging with interlaying of ease

overtly alert and vividly present

in the mystery of unfolding

everything abides in this natural play

of minds -

of self togetherness -

interconnected in universal love

Words from a teaching by Tarchin Hearn

72

Once you know where you come from
out there among the stars
our interconnectedness
our next peaceful breath
returns us to heaven

Enlightened.

The author;

Sam is my pseudonym, and nickname, which I prefer to be called. I use the nom-de-plume - Sam Eastwood as a writer.

Please feel free to comment on these poems and to offer a critique. If you wish to reproduce any of these poems please contact me directly at my email address.
sam@poems-by-sam.com
website www.poems-by-sam.com

Visit me at Facebook; Sam.Eastwood.777